Professional Excellence

Professional Excellence

EDUCATION IS THE KEY

Lynette Shelto-Johnson

Published by Publishing Push Ltd.

Copyright 2023 The Lynette Shelto-Johnson Book, London, England 2023

First published 2023

English translation 2023

Lynette Shelto-Johnson has asserted her right under the copyright design to be identified as the author of this book. This book is entirely a work of nonfiction.
This book is sold subject to the condition that it shall not by way of trade or otherwise be lent, resold, hired out or otherwise circulated other than that which it is published and without similar condition, including this condition being imposed on the subsequent purchaser.

Limited reference from the holy scriptures will be seen in this book.

978-1-80541-402-5 (paperback)
978-1-80541-403-2 (eBook)

Contents

Introduction 1
Love Is Powerful 3
Health Is Wealth: The Things We Eat 7
The Disadvantages of Not Knowing 13
Education: Professional Excellence 21
Climbing the Ladder of Success 27
Life in the Military 33
Knowing God Gives Inner Peace 37
The Beauty of Many Languages 43
Life Is Precious: The Weathers of Life 47
The Power of Prayer 55
End Times Prophecies 61
Survival for Today's Family 69
Hope for the World 79
Light at the End of the Tunnel 85
My Reasons for Writing This Book 89
Acknowledgements 91
Summary 95

Introduction

There has never been a successful or creatively gifted person who hasn't known failures, frustration or tough times. Times when money was scarce or non-existent. Times when he or she seemed out of touch with the rest of humanity. Times when fresh ideas and inspiration didn't flow, and times when physical or emotional handicaps seemed insurmountable. The hallmark of success is the ability to ride out these moments and still prevail. Frustration and disappointment, even sorrow, can lead to joy and prosperity. Often those who overcome the fiercest difficulties in education are the men and women who ultimately achieve the greatest triumphs and inspire us the most. For many discouraging hours will arise before the rainbow of accomplished goals will appear on the horizon.

Let me introduce myself before I let you into my amazing book. My name is Lynette Shelto-Johnson, and I was born in Guyana which is one of the most beautiful countries in the amazing Caribbean. I am a nurse by profession, now a registered nurse/registered care home manager and a writer in my spare time. Doing ministry work is also one of my callings from God. I am writing this little book from my home apartment in London.

Guyana is known to have six different races of beautiful people with a great diverse cultural history. The Caribbean is well known for its amazing sunshine and beautiful beaches, rivers and rainforest, and gold and diamonds.

There are so many things we may not have had the knowledge to know. Things we always sit and wonder about: how could this be possible and when could it be possible. The truth is, we may never be able to know until we ourselves embark on the pastures to know the unknown. My father used to say that knowledge is powerful and this I do believe. In my younger years, I was ignorant of the facts of many things but my curiosity of finding out the unknown brought me to a place where I experienced that knowledge is indeed powerful.

Allow me to take you through the avenues of professional knowledge as you sit back, relax and enjoy reading the things that increase our chances of great knowledge. This book has the ingredients to motivate you to dive deep into the path of knowledge which will make you excel in your professional excellence.

Love for ourselves, others and the world is the greatest knowledge we need for these trying and unprecedented times. Uncertain times are ahead of us.

Despite the perilous and uncertain times, love will triumph overall. God's grace and mercies are new each morning.

Fasten your seat belts. Here we go. Do enjoy the rolling contents of my amazing book. May God bless you and your family as you continue to love one another.

Love Is Powerful

True love is the most powerful thing I have ever known because God himself is love. Some people think of love in various ways, but love is rich, priceless, yet a hundred percent free. Some people will pay money to buy love but please do remember that no amount of money can buy love. True love must come from deep within your heart. This is why most relationships that were formed around money have now been broken because when the money is finished, the relationship fails to exist.

Relationships that were formed from true love mostly stand the test of time. Love endures many bad situations. Despite money being good for maintenance, many relationships with true love survive because love is powerful enough to keep the relationship fully grounded.

Those who live with true love within their hearts have learnt to easily forgive. Those who love give freely to help others, even if they are giving their last.

I experienced many times where I have given from the little I had and days afterwards I was blessed with double the portion of what I gave. Remember we give not to receive but we give knowing God will bless us in return.

The King James Bible spoke about the love of God. The Bible tells us that God so loved the world that he gave his only begotten son that whosoever believe in him shall not perish but shall have everlasting life. This type of love God demonstrated to us is a powerful and divine love.

There are husbands and wives who have shown great love to each other. Parents who have shown great love for their children and so on.

I have learnt from experience over the years that money can give us comfort, but money won't give us true happiness. There are some people who are rich, yet they are unhappy. Wealth without health brings unhappiness. Wealth without true love brings unhappiness.

Some people believe that money rules the world. Let me invite your mind back to 2020 when we were in the peak of the COVID-19 pandemic. Many of those people who had a love for money were not thinking much about money at that time. Everyone wanted to be with their families. Everyone wanted to make sure their families and friends were safe. I wasn't hearing a lot of talk about money because money did not mean so much during the pandemic. Everywhere was shutdown except for a few essentials shops to buy food.

The cinemas and theatres, football stadiums and so many other places like pubs were closed. Those businesses lost money while the people saved money because they spent less during the pandemic.

During this time, love was being shown in many ways. People were taking food to the elderly who couldn't get around. Families and friends were communicating frequently. Love was above money during the pandemic. This was a time when people realised how important love for families and friends was. People realised it was a time when money had no power as people were only praying and depending on the grace and mercies of God to get them through the pandemic safely. The love for life was more important than the love for money. Money will come and money will go but true love is powerful. It is here to stay. True love will always stand the test of time. True love will last forever.

Marriage was ordained by God. Some people may get married for various reasons, but it is always better to get married for love. Respect yourself and respect the person you are in the relationship with. Respect everyone. Please do not let the love for money destroy your relationship. Money is good and money can be bad when greed is involved. Always put love above money then money will eventually follow.

The world demonstrated a very high level of love during the pandemic. It is the same when there is a hurricane or earthquake or something severe.

It would be a great idea if the world could continue to demonstrate that high quality of care for one another and show love continuously. Then the world will be a better place to live in.

I love that little song that says, "Love in any language, straight from the heart. Moves us all together, never apart. And once we learn to speak it, all the world will hear. Love in any language, fluently spoken here." What a beautiful song that is.

The King James Bible tells us about loving our neighbours as ourselves. This should be an unconditional thing. We will make ourselves happy by making others happy. When God blesses you, share your blessings with others. Let the love continue to flow for others to feel that love.

I can remember when my mum and dad passed on. Money was far from my mind as sadness took over. The love of God and the love of family and friends gave us the comfort to stay strong. Love is more powerful than you and I could comprehend. The human mind could only imagine how powerful it is but love is of a superior and divine origin because love is of God. God is love and he loves you and I with an everlasting love. Let us continue to love one another always.

Health Is Wealth: The Things We Eat

The love of God is our greatest wealth. Even if we don't have good health, once we have love within our hearts, we have one of the greatest treasures which is an amazing gift from God.

Health is a great wealth as it gives us that inner peace of mind. It gives us emotional and physical strength. Having good health is the power of God and good health makes us happy.

When I was a young midwife, I was taught that health begins before the birth of someone. The gynaecologist would educate the pregnant mother about the nutritious foods she needs to eat, so she can maintain good health for herself and her baby. If the pregnant woman failed to eat a nutritious diet, then she could put her life and the life of her baby at risk.

This confirms that health maintenance begins before the birth of a baby and health maintenance stops when someone dies. It is an ongoing process which we must have in balance.

Having all the money in the world doesn't mean anything if you don't have good health. When someone is sick, that person does not think so much about the money they have. One of the main things on that person's mind would be to feel better.

This is a time when many people turn to God for help to heal them. This is a vital time when many people turn to God in prayer for help. Prayer is a powerful tool God gave to us so we can communicate with him. Some people only use prayers when they need help from God, but prayers should be continuous in good times and bad times.

After the birth of a baby, the mother, in her postnatal stage, still needs to have check-ups to make sure her body is returning to the normal pre-pregnancy process. The baby health checks and immunity vaccine treatments will also commence. This will continue as the child grows. Health maintenance is required throughout life. Just like no one is perfect, the same is true that no one is perfect where health is concerned. Even if we do not have major health issues, none of us can say that we have a hundred percent perfect health. Everyone can name something that is not quite right with their health. It could be just headaches, hay fever, or some of the easily managed illnesses. Whereas some people have conditions such as diabetes, high blood pressure, high cholesterol, lung conditions, heart conditions, kidney disease and so much more. These conditions call for strict diets along with other management plans your doctor will prescribe for you to follow. Any of these conditions can be life threatening if you do not follow the strict instructions on your doctor's treatment plan.

For example, diabetes is difficult to control as many people love sweet foods like cakes, ice cream and sugary drinks. It is vital to avoid such things with high quantities of glucose. If you are unable to avoid these things, try your best to reduce sweets in your diet to a greater extent. If you are on tablets or insulin, it is important that you stick to the treatment plan. Monitor your blood glucose levels as often as possible to determine if your treatment is working or if you are managing well on your diet.

For those of you with high blood pressure, this is a condition that can be difficult to manage in the world we are living in with the unprecedented and uncertain times. Nevertheless, stay on your medication plan. Avoid any stressors that will pave the way to increasing your blood pressure. Avoid salt in your diet. Try to exercise as much as you can. Talking walks will be good for your health and your mind. I live eight minutes away from work and I walk to work and walk back home. Taking in the morning fresh air is good for the mind.

Yoga or simply dancing in your home is a way of freeing up your mind. You will feel good about yourself, and it will help you to control your blood pressure. When I plan a concert at work, I usually take part in the concert activities. I usually place myself in the dance group as dancing is something that makes me feel good about myself. It helps me with my exercise plan, and it loosens up the stiff muscles.

Avoid foods with high cholesterol as high cholesterol is also a medium for high blood pressure. Take the yearly recommended cholesterol test. It will help you be able to control your cholesterol levels.

People with stomach problems should avoid spicy foods and avoid acidic drinks. These foods should not be taken during the night as the digestive system slows down during the night and the acid build-up in the stomach will be greater. If you do have stomach burns during the night, increase your water intake or drink a warm cup of milk which will help to neutralise the acid in your stomach. Your doctor may prescribe antacid suspension or may give you tablets such as omeprazole. It is important that you take good care of your stomach. See your doctor if the problems persist.

It is known that true happiness can be found deep within the heart. When your mind is happy, your heart will be happy.

It is also known that a person's appetite increases if they have a happy mind. If someone is unhappy, the appetite stimulant will eventually reduce, thus causing a reduction of food intake. The environment where we dine also plays a part in the appetite stimulating process. The presentation of the meal can determine the way our appetite works too. A poor environment and poor food presentation will inhibit a good appetite. The quantity of food during dining is also a factor to take into consideration as some people's appetites reduce when too much food is placed on the plate. The best option is to give a small portion of food, which is a great appetite stimulant.

The taste of the food is vital as this can determine a person's appetite and how much they eat. If you are cooking for someone, it is important to know the types of food the person likes to eat. Some people like a bland diet and other people don't. Some people like spicy diets. Some people like food without salt and tea without sugar and so on.

It is essential to know your body, know your health conditions and know what types of food are best for you. I know taste and flavour are important for diets but eating the right diet for your health is more important than the taste of what we eat.

Stay healthy. Stay happy.

The Disadvantages of Not Knowing

I have always known knowledge to be a powerful thing. It is something everyone should try to attain to the highest level. The more you know about things, the more you will be able to go through life doing things for yourself and helping others as well.

It can be very stressful when you can't do something because you lack the knowledge.

Many people spend endless amounts of money paying for simple things they don't know how to do. Try to learn how to do the simple things you pay to have done so you can save your money. Something as simple as calling someone to check your electricity if the lights go off. Let someone teach you how to check your electricity fuse box. Sometimes the electricity power is overloaded and one of the fuses might switch itself off. If you know how to turn that fuse back on, you don't need to pay someone to do that. Another thing is paying someone every year to unblock your kitchen sink. If you get into the habit of using sink clearing chemicals at least once a month, it will keep the drains clear and save you the money for a plumber.

Let us look at an example of people who may not know how to read or write. These people may not know how to count money either. If the shop owner wants to be unfair, they could give that person the wrong change when they go to buy groceries. If they continue to lack this knowledge, then it will be a disadvantage to the person throughout their life.

Some parents may not have the money to send their children to school. This would be a disadvantage to the children because they wouldn't get the relevant education to take them through life. These children will be unhappy knowing that their friends are going to school and getting the necessary education and they are unable to.

It is vital that every parent tries hard to make sure their children secure a sound education for their academic wellbeing. When the children are still in their young days, they may not understand the importance of a good education. As parents it is your duty to make this a priority. If you do not have money, seek help from family or friends and make sure your children go to school. The government education department may be somewhere you could seek help from. Do your best to give your children the best education possible.

You can also help to teach your children at home. Simply teaching them how to count money is important so when they go to the shop, they won't get back the wrong change. Teach them about farming if you have the knowledge. Fruits and vegetables are getting expensive so farming will help yourself and children to know how to farm to save spending.

Teach your children how to cook. The more you teach your children, the more they will be able to face the world with confidence. Your child may not have a higher education but teaching them how to cook could allow them to become one of the best chefs ever. Teach your children how to clean the house. You may never know, housekeeping may assist them in a foreign country while trying to develop themselves.

One of the worst things is to enter a meeting without knowing what is on the agenda. You would not be able to communicate effectively. You would be more prepared if you knew what to expect. There is a saying that if you fail to prepare, then you need to prepare to fail. Children need a good education before they leave school. Lack of knowledge is a disadvantage, especially a severe knowledge deficit.

Nothing will be able to stand in your way if you walk wisely. If you do not know the requirements and the tools to get you through education, it would not do you any good. To further your education, use whatever tools you have until you can get more of the required ones.

This is especially true for your daughters. Make sure they know a little of everything, such as cleaning the house and knowing how to cook, and make sure they have a sound education. Many women today stay in abusive relationships and abusive marriages because they do not have a sound education and are unable to go out and work on their own. Not having an education and being unable to get a job, some women go through emotional and physical abuse.

Women can go to sewing classes. They can go to cooking classes. Housekeeping classes, pastry and cake decorating classes. Find something to do, so that if you are in an abusive relationship, you can leave and go and get a job. You are beautiful and you can develop yourself once you believe in yourself and set your mind to it.

Even the men should ensure that they secure themselves with a sound education because sometimes the men too go through abusive relationships. Some women will only stay in relationships for money. This is why all relationships should be based on love which is the main thing.

Having the knowledge makes us aware of something.

My daughter and I went to Paris in 2018 by plane which was only a one-hour flight.

This year, in 2023, on the Easter weekend, the train tickets were more expensive than the plane tickets. Neither of us wanted to use the plane after hearing about the flying missiles from Putin and the Ukraine war, so we decided to take the train. I am not sure why the train was more expensive, but we just preferred the train than taking the plane. I was also happy to travel by train as it was only two hours and seventeen minutes. I told my daughter it would be a lovely journey because we would be able to see various places on our way to France.

Not forgetting that we both have never travelled to France by train before, we were lacking knowledge of what the journey would fully be like. When I purchased the train tickets, I did not read the details properly, so I did not know it was a mostly underground journey.

THE DISADVANTAGES OF NOT KNOWING

I do not like the underground train journeys, but my daughter Crystal does not have a problem with it as she used underground trains to two different universities for five years. My daughter loves to research things. I am not sure if she knew before that the train to France had to travel through the underground under the sea, but she only mentioned this after the train was on the way to France.

I, like a scaredy cat, feared the unknown. I began to think and imagine the train travelling under the sea. That was a horrible thought for me. I am not ashamed to say that I never really knew that information about England and France. My daughter said she only researched it when we were already on the train as I told her if I knew I would have taken my chances with the plane and the possible flying missiles. She said she did not know before.

Half of the journey was travelling through tunnels but travelling through the tunnel under the sea was about twenty-five minutes. It took forever but thank God when my daughter told me that her phone was getting signal again after we came out from the tunnel. She then said her phone was saying welcome to France. I breathed a sigh of relief because I knew that any other tunnel would not be under the sea. The seats we had were facing the opposite direction which made it a bit awkward.

When we entered France, we travelled about another hour before reaching the train station. There were no more scary tunnels. The scenery in France was beautiful.

We spent an amazing Easter weekend in Paris. The hotel, the boat cruise and the restaurants' food were all amazing. I did not even try to think about the return journey home through the tunnel under the sea. My daughter was laughing at me because I was fearful of the tunnel.

Anyway, you may be surprised if I tell you that our journey back to London with the same train travelling through the tunnel under the sea was a less scary journey for me. We had seats that were facing the direction the train was going and I had full knowledge of what to expect. I knew the tunnel only lasted twenty-five minutes, so I was praying for those twenty-five minutes to finish. For some reason the travelling back seemed faster than the going. It all boiled down to knowing what to expect.

Would I ever travel with the train to Paris again through the tunnel? Maybe I would, as it was not as bad as I first imagined. Eighty percent I would take the plane next time, as it is only one hour. Both planes and trains have their advantages and disadvantages.

I used my experience here, so you would understand how important it is to have knowledge of as many things as possible. I am sure you would agree that knowledge is vital for our survival in the world.

The knowledge of choosing the right words is incredibly important because they have the power to impact others in ways that can be positive or negative. When we speak, we can inspire, uplift and heal those around us, but we also have the potential to hurt or offend. Therefore, it's essential to choose our words carefully.

Words can have a profound impact on others, and they can even shape how people view themselves and the world around them. When we use positive and empowering language, we can lift people up and inspire them to be their best selves. On the other hand, when we use negative and hurtful language, we can cause people to feel discouraged and disheartened.

This is why it's important to always think about the impact that our words may have on others and to choose them carefully. By doing so, we can create a more positive and uplifting environment for ourselves and those around us. You have more power than you realise. So, don't be reckless with your words. Use that power responsibly.

Education: Professional Excellence

Education is vital for everyone. Education begins from birth. As silly as it may seem, we see parents speaking to their babies from birth. Even when the child is not able to comprehend, parents still speak to that child. As the child continues to grow, they begin to understand things gradually. Never feel that your child is too young to commence education.

There has never been a successful or creatively gifted person who hasn't known failures, frustration or tough times. Times when money was scarce or non-existent. Times when he or she seemed out of touch with the rest of humanity. Times when fresh ideas and inspiration didn't flow, and times when physical or emotional handicaps seemed insurmountable. The hallmark of success is the ability to ride out these moments and still prevail. Frustration and disappointment, even sorrow, can lead to joy and prosperity. Often those who overcome the fiercest difficulties are the men and women who ultimately achieve the greatest triumphs and inspire us the most.

Mothers go to children's clinics where the doctors will teach them how to care for their children. The children are given immunity vaccines and the doctors explain the purpose of the vaccines to the mothers. This is also a part of the education process for both mother and child.

When the child is old enough, the parents should enrol the child in school. The parents should take the responsibility to ensure that the child completes school. It is vital for the parents to attend school meetings to get updates regarding their child's progress in the school.

They should support the child at home by making sure they complete their assignments, and making sure they have a good breakfast before going to school. They should ensure that they have the necessary educational tools where possible to enable them to complete their studies.

Encourage your children to motivate them. When they pass their exams, give them little gifts of encouragement. If they fail a test, do not speak badly to them. Encourage them to work harder and do better next time. The words you speak to them can motivate them or demotivate them. Choose your words carefully.

Peer pressure can destroy the life of a child at school. Educate your children about peer pressure. Teach them that they don't have to adhere to peer pressure. They don't have to adhere and be forced into gangs. They don't have to be afraid of bullies. Teach them to be brave and bold enough to report any uncomfortable situations to the school office. If your children start accepting bad things in school, they will eventually get into trouble, or their education could be affected due to such things. A very sound education is good for both parents and children.

EDUCATION: PROFESSIONAL EXCELLENCE

Remember your role as a parent is to guide your children into becoming productive people, who will honour themselves and their community. Know that your child is learning your values by how you live, not by what you say. Just doing the right and decent thing can set the pace for others to follow. "Train up a child in the way he should go: and when he is old, he will not depart from it." This can be found in the King James Bible in Proverbs 22:6.

Education shouldn't stop at secondary school. People should try to achieve higher education where possible. Education only stops when you die.

I know of someone who graduated law school the same year as my daughter. That person was eighty-one years old. To attain professional excellence, you need to continue education and keep aiming for the sky.

According to my big sister Doris, it takes a village to raise a child. The community needs to work together for the good of the children. One person can make a difference, and everyone should try. The ability to change for the better in our own life and the lives of all our children starts with a heathy mind, body and spirit and a change of thoughts, communications and actions of our own self first. We do not have to be the person in authority to make a difference. I am not a person in authority, but we do, however, have to have a clear vision and be able to communicate that clearly with others. We need to go out and make a difference in our community. We do not need endless time and perfect conditions. We need to do things now and do them today. We can just do things for only about twenty minutes to help make a difference. There is no greater joy, no greater reward, than to make a fundamental difference in someone's life.

It is often through failures that success comes. Keep working hard. Failure is not failure unless you have not learnt nothing from it.

What we conceive in our mind, if we believe, we can achieve. The key to a dream is not to focus on success but significance and then the small steps and victories along your successful path. These will lead you on to greater meanings. The reaching of your goal should then be the beginning of another.

The path to educational success is not always straight. You may have gone the wrong way. You may have lost your way. You may have to make a U turn and come back and so on. What matters is that you took the first step to embark on the road to education, because education is the key to success as my sister Doris usually says to the children in her classroom.

God gives us opportunities. It is what we decide to do with those opportunities that defines us. Make every opportunity count as opportunities sometimes only come once and tomorrow is not a promise to anyone.

Some people would say aim for the stars. I love to say aim for the moon and if you fall you will land amongst the beautiful stars.

Part of doing something difficult is always believing that you can do it. If you would like to have an education, go out and get it. I know some people who work two or three jobs to acquire higher education. They had no regrets doing two or three jobs as it paid off.

Many of us dreamt of becoming one thing but the good Lord has blessed us with multiple things. It is good to have the knowledge of being able to do many things.

The value of a sound education is also a significant topic, highlighting the merit it adds to our lives. The importance of road safety is also emphasised, reminding us to be cautious and mindful when using the roadways. The safe use of the roadways in every country is vital to reduce the amount of road accidents, especially in the wake of a notable spike in road accidents across all countries.

Another interesting topic for our children is arts and crafts, which is a fun way to express creativity and relieve stress.

May God bless you all as you strive for professional excellence.

Climbing the Ladder of Success

Life is a continuous journey of uncertain times. Maybe you are at a crossroad in life where you don't know which road to take. Maybe you thought of taking one road, then you changed your mind and took another road. Life is sometimes about taking chances to see where life will take you.

It is always a good idea to take a pause, pray and allow God to help you make a wise decision when you are at a crossroad.

Many people start a business with a small amount of money not knowing if the business will be a success or not. It is always better to try to fail than to not try at all.

Speaking about climbing the ladder of success, this calls for determination. This calls for motivation, willpower and believing in oneself. Aiming for success is not an easy thing.

Some days it will feel like you are going down the ladder of success more than climbing up. You may feel like you have touched the bottom of the ladder.

In life it is not about how you fall but it is about how you get up, shake the dust off and rise to success with great strength. Rise without looking downwards. Most people keep looking down and this is what makes them miss the steps on the ladder and fall. Some people like to say aim for the stars. I like to say aim for the moon and if you fall you will still land amongst the beautiful stars. Be a star while climbing for success. Shine your light when climbing so you can help someone else climb that ladder of success. It could be financial success. It could be physical, emotional or spiritual success. It could be success in attaining good health. Shine your light. Some people like to reach the top of the ladder of success and may not want others to be in the same situation.

Success, fame and earthly glory is good to attain but it is also good to see others reach that stage of success. When we help others, we are helping ourselves. It will make us emotionally happy to see others being successful.

If you fail to prepare, then you must be prepared to fail. Getting to that stage of success you must believe in God and believe in yourself. Not knowing how you will get to the top of the success ladder is like unseen steps to victory. You must have a determined mind and a mindset that you can make it despite the unprecedented times. You must have resilience and maintain it if you would like to make it to the top. Resilience will keep you moving forwards and not backwards.

Don't be afraid of downfalls. Use them as stepping stones to your success.

Do not burn bridges on your way to success. You may never know if you will need that bridge to divert you on the road to success. In every climb, feel good about yourself and give thanks to God and those who help you along the way.

Some people may be on your road to success as a blessing. Some people may be on that road as some form of a lesson.

In every aspect of your climb, it is all in the puzzle to get you to the top of the success ladder. Be fair in every situation. Be kind in every aspect of success. Be grateful for all the help. Be forgiving in any wrong done to you. Enjoy every minute of life. Don't stress about it when things don't go your way because rain doesn't fall forever, and storm clouds always pass over. Keep thinking about that and you will know that once there is life, there is hope.

Sometimes a physical ladder may have missing steps. The same is with your life. You may feel alone sometimes and feel that you are not moving from the situation you may be in. Trust God and believe he can move you from a place of poverty to a place of comfort. Trust God that he can move you from the bottom of the ladder of spiritual darkness to the light of the top of the success ladder. It will either be emotional, physical, financial or spiritual. Believing in yourself plays a great role in the way you gain success in life. Keep moving.

Giving up shouldn't be an option. Many gold miners gave up just before hitting that rock of gold, leaving someone else to collect the reward of their hard work. Many times people give up too soon.

Sometimes it can be difficult to reach that place of success but with God, hard work and dedication, along with resilience, you can get there. I have been in a situation where I worked hard for years to get to the nurse manager position I have now. Sometimes I wanted to give up, but perseverance and hard work paid off. In my book, giving up wasn't an option.

Do not compare yourself to others. Everyone is unique in their own way. It is good to focus on your own journey. Everyone's success comes in various ways. Paying too much attention to others and what they are doing will make you lose focus on your own climb for success. You should only focus on someone if they need your help which you should render.

You should keep aiming for your goal. You do not need to stop on your way to prove yourself to anyone. Keep moving towards your goal. Try to be the best version of yourself and not someone else's version. Adopt a mindset that allows you to be free from any form of pressure.

Focus on your own growth and happiness. Concentrate on your goal and what you require to meet that point of success.

When you gain success, do not be afraid of sharing your knowledge with others. This is a world where we should love one another. Share your dreams with others. Share your success with others. Share your knowledge. Some people are afraid of others being more successful than they are. Don't worry about that. Keep doing well and your cup will keep running over.

Before you start climbing the ladder, I guess you may have asked God for guidance and knowledge. When you reach the top of the ladder of success, do remember to give thanks to the one who got you there. God is good.

Remember to thank everyone who was supportive of you. You couldn't have done it alone. Celebrate your success and celebrate the success of others. Be happy with yourself and be happy about others. When I was a child, I first heard about creeping before you walk. We all, at some point in our lives, had to creep before we walked. Wherever you start climbing the ladder of success, make every step up the ladder count. Even if you don't see the other step up the ladder, keep climbing. Let hope, faith and love motivate you to find the next step. Work hard to get to your goal of success and let your dreams turn into reality by demonstrating professional excellence.

To achieve your academic goals, it takes a commitment change and a deeper commitment to grow.

Many great achievements were accomplished by tired and frustrated people who kept on praying and working hard.

Someone by the name of Tammy once said, "A journey of a thousand miles begins with a single step." It is a famous Chinese proverb. A Guyanese proverb is one of, "We must learn to creep before we walk." Another powerful piece of advice is to think carefully before you speak. Harsh words can hurt or even destroy someone. Let kind words pave your steps. Our actions determine our personality. Let our lifestyle be a silent and good teaching example to others. They can learn something from your smile.

A simple smile and kindness can make a sad person happy. These are all a part of the education agenda. They can help you live a happy life.

Stars shine, so be a star and bless someone else's life.

Life in the Military

Life is not a bed of roses but a life of love and dedication to your country. It is a life of loyalty to your country. It is a life of making sacrifices of your time with family and friends to serve your country. I know this is not an easy thing for military personnel. Leaving your families and friends and not knowing if you will be able to see them again must be a terrible feeling. Going to the battlefront is probably one of the scariest things but soldiers give up everything to serve their countries.

I salute every soldier who serves their country for a good cause. Respect to them all. Especially those veterans who must live every day of their lives remembering all the good and bad times they encountered during the war times.

Not knowing about something, one can only imagine. Knowing about something or having a glimpse of it makes one understand things from a better perspective.

Years ago in Guyana, nurses had to undergo four months of military training before entering nursing school. I remember it like it was yesterday because I was one of those nurses who underwent months of military training. It was packed and difficult. Having to get up at 5 a.m. and run miles with rifles was difficult but it taught me determination. The jungle mock wars with the self-loading machine guns taught me jungle survival. Going to the firing range taught me about being exact and being quick with handling a rifle. Going to the drill square taught me discipline.

Living in the dormitory taught me how to keep a house tidy. When the military cargo plane crashed, it taught me about eating less and being contented. It taught me survival game. When the water cut off, we were being taught how to use a limited water supply.

We were instructed not to go down to the river when the water cut off but that was one of the instructions that most of the military personnel rarely followed. The river was full every day until the water returned through the pipe. I was amongst the cadets in the river who didn't followed instructions. The river water was refreshing.

Having a mock war was difficult yet fun for us but what about those soldiers who go through live nonfiction combat? Many of them never make it back home. Children are left without fathers or mothers due to the wars claiming their lives. Having to live in tunnels, caves, jungles and other uncomfortable places to monitor the enemies' situations can never be fun. Despite knowing that, the soldiers took up that job to protect us. There may be many days where they go without food while we comfortably eat our daily meals. The military life is hard, but those soldiers decided to serve their countries. They are brave men and women. They are heroes.

My daughter and I went to Paris and stood by the memorial site. There were names of many soldiers who did not make it back home. These were soldiers who faced guns and bullets for their countries. Soldiers whose children, wives, husbands, fathers, mothers, brothers and sisters never got the chance to see them return home alive. Yet some people show no respect for soldiers. Wars are terrible situations to be in, yet the world continues with wars and rumours of wars. Let us treat our soldiers with respect and be thankful for them for defending our countries.

Let us also show respect and be thankful to the policemen and women who are also protecting our societies. I salute all the people in the different types of military departments too for looking out for the good of the people.

I pray for the day when the world can live as one with no wars. When we all can live as one people, one nation and one destiny. Love is the answer but in the society of today, hatred seems to be more prevalent than love.

Knowing God Gives Inner Peace

Since I was a child, my parents taught my siblings and I that if we know God, we will experience what peace is. I am writing this book in my small cosy apartment home in London remembering the teachings of my parents. My parents have both passed on, but the teachings of God and the peace of peace remains with me and my siblings. We will forever be grateful to them.

My book is about knowledge and professional excellence and the genre is education. I based this chapter on God and inner peace because I know we all need that inner comforting peace of God to go through the earthly dramas that are unfolding before our very eyes. Every day we listen to the news, there is something new about crime. Something new about war, maybe an earthquake or tornado and so much more for the human mind to comprehend.

How can we stand the trying times? How can we stand the test of time? How can we stand the shaking and the shifting times? How can we manoeuvre and get over the difficulties of the unprecedented and uncertain times? The answers are within our hearts and minds.

The answer is to know God, trust him and walk with God. Ask him to direct your path and the paths of your family, friends and others out there. The grace and mercies of God are new each morning so accept them. Embrace them. Enjoy them and give God thanks, praise, honour and glory, for his love towards us is unconditional.

One fundamental truth you should know is that the truth of God endures forever.

The best truth we can know is that love triumphs over all because God himself is love. Once we have love, we have the best education this earth can teach us.

Millions of people have degrees, but many do not have love within their hearts. They look down at people with disrespect. It doesn't matter how much education you have, if you do not know God and if you do not have love within your heart, you shall not have inner peace. You will continue to feel that something is missing from your life. Millions of people do not have an earthly education, but they speak as if they are highly educated because they have the love of God within their heart. Some of these people will speak to you with professional excellence. This is because they demonstrate love to everyone as they travel around the world. Love is the most powerful thing, and it gives us that inner peace of God.

Religion can sometimes be very disruptive as some people focus more on religion than focusing on sharing the love of God. This can be found in every religious organisation. We have heard of religious wars. God does not want war; God wants us to live in peace and love. It doesn't matter which religion you are from, if you do not know God and have love within your heart, you will never experience the inner peace of God.

You may ask me why I am speaking about God if I am writing a book about knowledge. The answer is simple. God created us and he knows everything about us. He knows everything about the world and everything therein. For us to attain great knowledge and gain professional excellence, God is the greatest person to have that close relationship with to attain such heights. To reach the top of the ladder of success, we need God in our daily lives. Once we have that inner peace of God, we can overcome anything on the emotional and mental side. Once we pray and trust God, we can get through any difficulties to achieve our educational goals.

Sometimes failures may come. This is when you and I may fall. It is not about the falling down in life, but it is about the way we rise to victory. It is about the way we rise to the ladder of success. Demonstrating love every day and having the inner peace of God will surely put you in a place of professional excellence.

Throughout my academic career, I prayed to God and trusted him to take me through to a level of my career where I would be able to be comfortable in life. I didn't pray for great earthly riches. What I do know for sure is that God has taken me to a level of higher heights than what I prayed for. I have chosen to glorify God in my messages at church, my messages at home, at work, on social media and my messages in writing my books. The inner peace of God is making me do these things.

Am I a great writer? The answer is no. Nevertheless, before I do my writing, I pray and ask God to direct my thoughts as I write so my messages can inspire and motivate as many people as possible. I made a choice to write my inspiring and motivating books because the world needs such messages for the uncertain times we are living in.

One of the things that motivated me during the pandemic was looking at my daughter studying her law books. I wondered how she was able to do such intense studying during the peak of the pandemic when the news was talking about thousands of deaths daily. I had to keep reminding myself that my daughter was able to do it with prayer and trust in God. My daughter studied throughout one of earth's greatest pandemics but by God's strength and mercy and by his grace, my daughter, along with many others, graduated from law university. My daughter does not go to church as often as I do but she reads the Bible more often than I do and she prays, and she strongly believes in God to get her through things.

I can remember when my daughter was at university doing her English degree. There was an attempted bombing on the underground train she used to go to the university. I can remember she was afraid to go back on the underground train. The underground train used to get her to the university in fifty minutes. The buses took almost two hours.

My daughter Crystal took the buses for about three days, but she found them to be very stressful due to the long travelling time. She told me she would travel back on the underground train and if she had to die from bombing then let it happen because the bus was taking too long. Crystal completed her English degree and graduated. Thank God there were no more bombings on the underground train.

For you and I to brave it despite the difficulties of life, we need the love and inner peace of God to take us through them. Once we have these things, we will be able to go through the storms of life knowing that God will take us through the fire untouched.

Self-control is strength, calmness is mastery. You must get to a point where your mood doesn't shift based on the insignificant actions of someone else. Do not allow others to control the direction of your life, and don't allow your emotions to overpower your intelligence.

Let us always remember that rain doesn't fall forever, and storm clouds always pass over. There is always a silver lining behind every dark cloud. Trust in yourself. Trust in God. Your victory shall come.

Keep away from negativity. Stay close to positivity. Avoid people who like to gossip and speak ill things about others. Always respond to them with positive comments. Think on these things.

The Beauty of Many Languages

I travelled many times in my younger days to many countries. I still do travel but not as much as when I was younger as I don't like long-distance travelling.

Travelling to various countries gave me the privilege of hearing different types of languages. When younger, I used to think of another language as confusing as I didn't understand them.

As I am older now, I have grasped the importance of knowing other languages which is vital for us as we travel to different countries.

As an older lady, I find different languages to be like beautiful music to my ears. I love to listen to different languages, but not knowing what I am hearing can be a bit frustrating to me sometimes. This is why knowing is important. This is one of the reasons for choosing the subtitle *Education Is the Key* for my book.

It is good to know at least the basics in as many languages as possible. This will help you be able to understand some things during your travels around the globe.

My daughter Crystal and I visited Paris twice. What a beautiful and amazing place. Our second visit for Easter this year was more enjoyable than our first visit in 2018. We finished our visit with a boat cruise. The sightseeing was amazing. The restaurant food was delicious.

Thankfully, we both had a small amount of knowledge of French. I lived in St Lucia for fifteen years working as a nurse. My daughter Crystal was born in St Lucia. St Lucia speaks broken French and we learnt some French there which was helpful for our trips to Paris. So, it wasn't that frustrating not understanding the French language.

When I first went to St Lucia in 1991, I can remember that there were many times where I couldn't understand what the neighbours were saying as most of the elderly folks were speaking broken French. Thankfully, I was given a nursing job at Victoria Hospital which is in the city of Castries. There I worked for many years. People mostly speak English in the city which was lucky. The hospital staff speak English, but the doctors and nurses will also speak French to the elderly who only speak French.

My little sister Nickie and my other sister Jennifer learnt the broken French language better than I did. I always enjoyed listening to the broken French language.

The first time I heard someone say "we", I thought it meant us. But it was *"oui"* which means yes in broken French.

It is so fulfilling to know other languages. It can help us to understand people who speak languages different from what we speak.

We may find English easy to understand but another person who speaks another language will find it difficult. My father told me that the English language is one of the most difficult languages to speak and I do agree. We who speak English sometimes find it difficult to speak. Even people from English-speaking countries sometimes say the wrong thing or find it difficult. This is why when English-speaking students do exams, they may make many mistakes. English is a beautiful but difficult language. When reading my book, you may pick up a wrong English statement as no one is perfect where the English language is concerned.

I wonder what would happen if we ever put all the languages together. Anyway, it is just a thought as we don't want it to be like the Tower of Babel where the people wanted to build the tower to reach God. Many of you may know this Bible story where God caused confusion and made the people speak in different languages so they couldn't understand each other. As a result, they couldn't continue to build the tower. They didn't pray to God before starting the tower. God knew they couldn't reach him through a tower.

My daughter and I bought our tickets to travel to Barcelona for summer this year as our flights were cancelled at the beginning of the pandemic.

My daughter knows a little Spanish from school, and I also learnt some Spanish at school. Do I remember anything much? The answer is no but at least I still have a little knowledge about the basics. This will help us with our trip to Barcelona. My daughter has visited Spain before, last year in 2022, and told me how amazing it is. I want to see for myself.

PROFESSIONAL EXCELLENCE

I can remember visiting Puerto Rico for a few days many years ago when I was living in St Lucia. Despite knowing a tiny bit of their language, it was still difficult and frustrating not being able to understand most of what they were saying.

Kindness is a language that the deaf can hear and the blind can see.

Always encourage your children to learn different languages. It will help them as they travel around the world.

Life Is Precious: The Weathers of Life

It is very important to know what the daily weather will be. Not knowing could be dangerous. Many people listen to the news every morning to know what type of day it will be. Will it be a sunny day, a rainy day, a windy day, or a cloudy day?

This information is vital to know before we leave our homes. For countries with a cold climate, we need thick coats for the cold temperatures. For tropical countries, we need clothing to keep us cool.

It is the same with our lives. Some days are happy days. Some days are not so happy days. Some days are sad days. Some days there may be disappointments. Some days we will have successes. Some days we will have failures. Some days we will fall and some days we will rise for the better.

What is important to know is that life has ups and downs. It is not about how we fall; it is about how we rise to success that matters.

Once there is life, there is hope. Some people were way down in life, but they did not give up. Many of those people own their own business etc. Some people did not have any education. Some of those people went all out to gain an education, of which some of those people have jobs in higher offices. Do not worry too much about where your life situation is now. Once you have life and strength, there is always hope that things will get better.

Nothing in life is permanent. There is always change.

You may be in a situation where no one is looking in your direction. You may feel that life is unfair to you. Families and friends might be too busy and do not have time for you. Stay strong and continue to focus on your goals in life. Miracles happen when you least expect them. Keep working hard. Keep believing in yourself. If there are gaps in your knowledge, keep climbing the education ladder.

Always remember, it does not matter how much you achieve, always remain humble. Always remember to continue to show kindness to everyone you meet. Do not let any bad situations change your good character.

When you are feeling down, know that this too shall pass. When things are not going your way, this too shall pass. Time is precious, so enjoy every second of it.

Yesterday is history. Some memories are good, and some are bad. Never worry about what you must do, everything will fall into place at the right situation and the right time. Tomorrow is a mystery. Today is a gift and that is why we call it the present.

God is our provider and our protector. He is our everything. God is the breath of life. God will stand by us. He will help us through. When we have done all we can do and we cannot cope, God will see us through. He will fight our fights.

I am grateful for the blessings. I am grateful to be me. I am grateful to be alive. I am grateful to be healthy. I am grateful to be breathing.

Speaking about constant change in life, I will share a story with you. I will never forget reading this amazing story of an elderly woman and her husband.

The bank gave them a few days to vacate their home as they could not come up with the owed money. The days they were given to leave their home came and went. The time was over, so to speak. The doorbell rang and the woman answered the door. A tall man was standing there.

At first, she thought it was the man from the bank visiting to ask them to leave. Instead, it was a man who knew the lady from his younger days.

She fearfully asked, "Who are you?"

The man responded by asking her if she remembered him. He said his name and she suddenly remembered him and began to smile.

She said, "Yes, I do remember now."

Her husband at the same time called out and asked her who it was, and she told him.

The rich business-like man told her that he had heard of her problems about the bank and her house. He said he was there to help her. He gave her three thousand dollars. She was happy and received the money with thanks.

The man told her that he had another surprise for her. He had some friends who also had known the lady from her school days as she was a teacher. She helped every one of those friends in some way or the other for the better. They all gave her a cheque with a large amount of money. The lady and her husband were so surprised, and very thankful. Due to this act of kindness from those people she taught in her younger days, she was able to keep her home.

This confirms to us that our situations in life can change just like the weather. Today can be rainy and tomorrow can be sunny. This is what happened in this amazing story I just shared with you.

This is how far acts of kindness can go. They can go for minutes, hours, days, weeks, months or years. In this case, the kindness for that teacher went for years.

The good we do to others can be repaid to other families and friends. Kindness is powerful.

Being humble and kind is a divine knowledge everyone should have. Patience and faith are also worthwhile.

Some people go through years of waiting to have children after getting married. This is a very emotional time for families having to go to the gynaecologist to go through various tests. This can be a mentally frustrating thing.

When every test proves that nothing is wrong, there is no other choice than to have faith and hope in God. Some women go through frustrating times going through miscarriages. These can be dark times in the lives of families.

I was in a similar situation as I am one of those women who went through some dark emotional years of sadness due to three miscarriages. The thought that I would not be able to give birth to a child was unbearable. The thought that I was too old to have children was playing on my mind. The gynaecologist completed all types of investigation and came up with nothing wrong. He suggested that maybe I waited too long to have children.

I continued to trust God. I continued to have faith and hope. One year later, I gave birth to my daughter. Thank the good Lord. My daughter is now twenty-six years old.

As the saying goes, who feels it, knows it. When we can relate to a certain situation or experience, then we can really and truly understand what another person is going through.

When the doctor's treatment does not work, or the tests are showing all normal, there is no other option than to pray, hope, have faith and patience, and trust the will of God. On the other hand, there are some women who never have any children, but they accept life as it is for them.

It is important that we all understand and have the knowledge that we are all different in our ways and genetic make-up, but we are all one in God.

We all go through different situations in life. We are all on this life journey, but we are not all travelling in the same boat. Life is precious and we need to learn to live within life's given situations. The same way we adopt ourselves to the different seasons such as winter, spring, summer and autumn. We should always keep hope alive. Always hope for a better tomorrow.

PROFESSIONAL EXCELLENCE

What is important is that we stay humble, kind and loving in any situation and any position we may have in life. One very important thing to remember daily is that every day is a gift, and that is why we call it the present. Tomorrow we can only hope for being a better person each new day.

When I was a young girl growing up, I prayed to be a nurse and one of the best nurses possible. I worked hard to acquire my goals in life. My dreams became a reality and I acquired more than I prayed for. This I usually call blessings with overflow.

What we all need to remember is that sometimes our prayers take longer to be answered. Our dreams and goals sometimes appear to be taking longer to accomplish. Faith and hope are fully required during such times.

In my first book *The Valley to the Mountain*, I wrote about being a serial manager. This is when I was promoted to acting nurse manager three times in three different workplaces. All three times I was unfairly treated. All three times I was not given the full manager's position.

I kept faith and hope alive after praying. Seven years ago, I was promoted to a full registered nurse manager at my present job. I have always learnt that giving up should never be an option.

Giving up on our education too, especially higher education, should not be an option. The more education we attain, the better chance for us to get a good job.

LIFE IS PRECIOUS: THE WEATHERS OF LIFE

Do not give up on your dream career. Sometimes in our adult life, we can also have dreams of other careers. I have dreams of being a writer and a counsellor. I have faith and hope that one day by God's grace I will be a professional writer. I love counselling, which I do daily, but not on a professional level. I counsel people every day for free in various situations.

I use my experiences to help people understand that situations can change once they keep hope alive.

There are different types of weather and I have seen so many storms in my life. We must learn how to exercise patience as we pray and wait for the storm to be over. God is good and his grace and mercies are new each morning. There are so many people who are weathering a storm right now. We can only depend on God to save us, that we can once again see that beautiful rainbow and the sunlight that will follow. For many discouraging hours will arise before the rainbow of accomplished goals will appear on the horizon.

The Power of Prayer

Praying is one of the best weapons God gave us to protect ourselves spiritually, emotionally and physically. Prayer is a powerful gift that helps us to communicate with God on the spiritual realm. Praying to God gives us that inner peace of security knowing he hears us when we pray. God always answers prayers. God likes it when we use prayers to communicate with him, but sometimes he delays answering our prayers. Try to cultivate a habit of praying in your home. If you are going to a school that does not pray before the lesson starts, you can still offer a word of prayer to God before the lesson begins. It should be the same when you go to work. Pray before you start your working day. Do not forget to pray before leaving your home. Ask God for protection and guidance, especially those who are driving. Ask God to be your eyes and your ears as some folks drink and drive.

Prayers help you to pass your exams. Prayers help you to be healed in Jesus' name emotionally, physically and spiritually. Many people who were suffering from addiction were healed through the power of prayer.

I went through lots of difficult situations but faith in God along with trust and prayers got me through those difficult times.

Family morning and evening prayers are good. Opening our classrooms with prayers is good. Opening our daily chores and our jobs with morning prayers is also good. Praying before we leave home for protection. Praying before driving, asking for protection on the roadways. Prayers changes things. Prayer is protection over our lives.

As I write this book, the true story came to my mind of when dozens of people gathered at Jacksonville Beach to pray Hurricane Irma away. Many turned to their faith to help weather the storm. This was in 2017. As anxiety increased, with the hurricane on its path, many trusted in their faith and God. The people on that day prepared for the storm but prayed that the storm would pass over. With the strong faith I have, I was praying and trusting that God would answer the prayers of the people and indeed he did.

Having the knowledge of the power of prayer and having the faith in the power of prayer are two different things. It is important to have both as both are needed for answered prayers.

I remembered the biblical story of the Red Sea crossing as I waited in 2017 to see what would be the outcome of that beautiful picture on the beach. The beautiful picture of dozens of people praying on Jacksonville Beach can be found on the internet. It was a Thursday evening as the people stood on the beach looking out to the sea praying to God, singing songs of praise. They prayed with outstretched hands asking God to push the hurricane out to sea. They comforted each other, saying do not be afraid, God will push the hurricane out to sea. Many churches and other groups accepted the emergency call for prayers and joined in. The King James Bible tells us that we have the power to pray and ask the storm to quiet down, and that is what those people did. The people did not want any further destruction to their land.

This amazing story was shared throughout the entire media in September 2017 regarding the Florida beach praying group. God has amazing ways of saving his people and yes, he did.

It is the same with when you are going to take any exams. You may pray asking God for success. When you have goals in mind and you want your dreams to come true, many people pray for success.

From my personal experience, I believe in the power of prayer. This is one great knowledge I have accomplished throughout the years.

I had some doubting experiences. One was not having money to travel to see my mum when she was sick years ago, but miraculously God sent tax returns into my account just on time for me to purchase a plane ticket. I was speechless when this happened, but then I remembered it was my prayer and the power of God.

The next personal experience I had I wrote about in my first book and briefly mentioned earlier on in this book. When I was thirty-three years old, the gynaecologist told me I may not have children. I prayed frequently and one year afterwards, I gave birth to my beautiful daughter. Having education on the knowledge of prayers is powerful.

Giving God praise and thanks every morning for life, everyone and everything should be the first thing for the day. We should not let negative vibes disturb our minds. Avoid listening to negativity. Some people use negative messages for their morning devotions. Let praise and worship to God be our morning vibes.

If we don't have anything good to say to inspire people, the best thing is silence. Those who share negative messages in the early morning and use them to pave their mornings will have negativity follow them throughout the day. If everyone shared positive thoughts, then the world would be a better place.

People's lives can be hindered by their attitudes and the negative messages they share with the world. These things will have negative consequences to these types of people.

Be kind. Be humble. Let your smile be genuine. It will brighten someone's day.

Whatever people dish out in their conversations and messages can give you an idea as to who those people are. To make the world a better place, let your contributions be positive and not negative.

If you are unhappy, try to brighten up your life and don't make others unhappy. Let us share positive words.

I saw a message from my sister Doris on Facebook speaking about being careful with the words we say to others. Words can make people happy, and words can hurt people.

Most people who write and say negative comments are mostly those people who are unhappy. Let us pray for them that God will grant them inner peace and love will flow within their hearts. Some mornings when I open social media, I see some heart-warming messages. Some mornings, the first thing might be a negative message. Our thoughts and minds will go with us throughout the day. What will yours be? Negative or positive? Think on these things.

There are some people who are kings and queens of negative thoughts and attitudes. You still have a personal choice to brighten someone's day or let your negative thoughts and negative messages pave your day. You can let positive attitudes brighten other's day.

It is time to ignite our spiritual faculty of faith as the substance of all things hoped for, and the evidence of things not seen. We are blessed to have within us an unshakeable faith that moves mountains. As we exercise our faith, we build a firm foundation on which to stand.

We trust that God is going to calm the storms of our lives. I allow myself to move with the stream. I am focused, I remain humble, and know that I will arrive safely to shore with God as the beacon. Each day presents an opportunity to prove this powerful promise: "What things soever ye desire, when ye pray, believe that ye receive them, and ye shall have them" (Mark 11:24). When I ask, the universe always answers, and through faith, I receive. No matter what the situation, I trust the process and surrender the outcome. Yes, I am standing on faith, and I shall not be moved. We acknowledge that God is alive, he is watching, his eyes are in every place. Please take all the necessary precautions to keep yourself and family safe during these uncertain times. The times are unpredicted. Pray without ceasing for the times are uncertain.

May God bless us all as we continue to inspire one another.

End Times Prophecies

Since I was a child, I have been hearing about end times prophecies. These things I read about in the King James Bible.

We can see that wars are still around the globe. The Ukraine war has been going on for more than a year and is still ongoing even now in 2023. Let's not forget this war commenced not long after a Christmas celebration. Not long after the dawn of a new year. Let's not forget the Ukraine war began when the COVID-19 pandemic was not fully over. I also remember that the war commenced in deep winter. This is what I consider true physical and emotional trauma for those involved and the world at large. The entire world was affected by this war and is still being affected due to the high rise of fuel prices.

Families were displaced. Families lost loved ones in the war. Soldiers on both sides died in large numbers, leaving families to mourn their deaths. Who would have thought or imagined that a war would have broken out in deep winter, just after the Christmas celebrations and the dawn of a new year? Who would have thought that people were thinking of war during a killer virus COVID-19?

The Ukraine war reminded me of the Gulf War, World War I and World War II. Families stayed in underground settings for months. Sometimes with no food or water. Some people did not know where their families were or if they were still alive. This was indeed a nightmare and still is. People are still not safe as it is still unsafe to move around in Ukraine due to unsafe grounds even now in 2023.

Families are in different countries now since their homes were destroyed in the war. People are unable to return to the place they once knew as a peaceful and beautiful haven.

As I write this book, there are also wars in so many other countries. Religious wars, political wars, wars for money, wars for so many other things.

Since I was a child growing up, so many people I knew have passed on. We all will die someday. I still cannot comprehend why people fight for various things. We came into this world with nothing, and we shall leave this world with nothing, except our good deeds and love for God and others, or our bad deeds. The choice should be ours on how we would like to leave this world.

We are living in perilous times. A time of uncertainty. A time when our homes and the roads are no longer safe. Praying ceaselessly is very important. Pray for yourself, your families, your friends and the world at large.

Earthquakes are prevalent also around the world. Buildings are crumbling in earthquakes like when cake crumbles.

Global warming is more evident as the weather is getting more unpredictable before our very eyes. Floods are so prevalent and remind me of the days of Noah in the biblical story. Brazil recently had a terrifying flood that claimed the lives of many people. The rain does not have reason anymore. Hurricanes do not have season anymore. Everything is unpredictable.

The world is going into a stage where some people love money more than they love others. The world is in a state where some people see right as wrong and wrong as right. It is a scary thing to see the way the world is moving at a fast pace to change the system.

Electronic scams are on the increase. Online scams are on the increase. There are scams at the ATM. Scams with some bike riders snatching people's phones. Please do not drop your bank cards as not everyone will hand it in to the bank like the old days.

Please be careful with responding to text messages because scammers are using your responses to access your phone details.

Fires are on the rise. Sometimes it is difficult to get rid of the fire in high-rise buildings. People are losing their lives from apartment fires.

Floods are on the rise. Global warming seems to be getting worse.

Tornadoes are more prevalent in places such as America and other countries. Crime is on the increase. Gun shootings are on the rise around the globe. Kidnapping is on the rise. People are moving and flowing around the world to find a better life. The cost of living is going up drastically. People's hearts are full of fear of the unknown of the future. Children are ruling parents. Children are beating teachers in schools. Some younger children have no respect for the elderly.

Sometimes the self takes over and we put pride before the goal. Sometimes we should help people for kindness and not for fame.

We should focus on the importance of maintaining a close relationship with God and communicating with him frequently to the significance of staying safe and healthy.

It is important that we stay humble and kind to one another. Being humble is divine knowledge. Patience and faith are worthwhile for the end times.

Problems will come but what is important is for us to keep love, faith and hope alive for the times ahead.

God can use the smallest child to the oldest person to spread his word.

He can use the poor and he can use the rich. He can use the smallest of animals to teach us how to live in love and unity.

We should clean our spiritual lives the same way we clean our house, our gardens, our cars and our place of work.

It is very important that we make use of the gifts God gave to us.

It does not matter who we are, where we came from, our nationality, or our colour, we can all share love for the world to help the world be a better place.

Let us all work hard to put away the things that are stopping us from entertaining love in our hearts. Things such as hatred, grudges, greed, jealousy, etc.

I pray that many people heal from the things they don't speak about.

We plan to follow God and do good when everything is better. There is a problem in telling God to wait on our time. We should follow God always and put him first as he controls everything. He owns tomorrow and only he knows what tomorrow will bring.

Our main goal is to follow God and share love and the news of salvation to a lost world.

Sometimes we just need a reminder that we are all visitors to this time, this place, and we are just passing through. Our purpose here is to learn, to grow, to love, and then we return home. Somewhere at the back of our minds we know that it is true; here is not our permanent home. So, let us appreciate each moment and find happiness, not in another place, but this place. Not for another hour, but this hour. As we opened our eyes this morning, the creator of this universe has granted us the privilege of seeing yet another beautiful day. Give him all the praise and all the glory for this moment. As you and I open our eyes, we do not complain about anything or anyone. We are blind towards the outcome of this day. It's a must that we lean on his guidance, and just be thankful for our spared life and that of our family, friends and strangers. Be grateful for today. Today is the present and that is why it is a gift.

We're seeing signs the world cannot ignore in 2023. I watched the news on the powerful earthquake that hit southern Turkey and Syria. Rescuers were racing to pull out survivors from beneath the rubble after a devastating quake ripped through leaving destruction, loss of so many lives, and debris on each side of the border.

That quake struck before sunrise, so I can imagine most of the people were in bed, sleeping.

This made me remember when we experienced slight tremors when I was living in Castries in St Lucia. I felt the house shake for a few seconds. I was fearful, but it was nothing compared to what we are seeing in Turkey. Now I question myself, are we in anyway prepared for disaster?

It can strike anywhere at any time. Disasters are indiscriminate and may be in any form, such as a hurricane, tornado, flood, fire, hazardous spill, earthquake, volcanic eruption, or man-made event.

It can hit suddenly and without warning, forcing people to go days without necessities, loss of lives, or evacuating from your homes. I don't know if we have sessions or discussions on disaster preparedness in schools, homes, youth groups and so on.

Preparing for disasters saves countless lives. The need to be prepared has become clearer now than ever. There should be training and we should equip hundreds of volunteers to work with communities for people to understand the needs of those most at risk. Parents should also grab the opportunity to teach their children at home.

We should set up early warning systems so communities can take early action before a disaster hits. Disaster preparedness is the smartest thing to do. Setting up actions is an investment in preparation now, rather than waiting for something to happen. We need to be always prepared. There are so many signs and prophecies showing that all is not well under the heavens. The world is in tribulation times. We need to stay strong and be prepared for the uncertain times ahead.

Survival for Today's Family

The family today needs lots of love and togetherness to stay together in love and unity. Let us look at some of the things we can do to increase hope for the families of today.

First, it is a big challenge for families to maintain a healthy, strong and happy relationship. Families are humans and despite working hard to build better relationships, our failings sometimes make it difficult to develop and sustain a healthy and happy family.

However, once there is life, there is hope for families. Determination, commitment and dedication should always be the focus of maintaining a healthy family relationship.

Learning to overcome negative attitudes is a good stepping stone to a successful family relationship. Learning to forgive one another of any wrong doings is also another way to stay on the right track.

God ordained marriage because it also helps to sustain the family and give some stability to the family today.

Effective communication within the family is vital and it is a beautiful and powerful thing. Effective communication is a special skill, and it is one of the best tools to prevent the breakdown of the family.

A home with a large family needs more communication exchange to keep the home from conflicts. God made the family, and he ordained marriage from the beginning.

The family should think more about giving to each other rather than getting from each other.

The great outdoors is wonderful for families to spend time together. Going to the park together, going to church together, going to the cinema together, theatres, football games, restaurants, gardens, travelling and so much more.

Families can try to watch an evening movie at home together, pray together and speak about good memories together. These are all ways of binding the family together.

The future and its uncertainty with all the bills going up is not easy for most of the families, especially large families.

Raising a child today is more difficult but teaching your children the right thing will pave the way for them to live a good life.

Families need hope for the unknown. Teaching your children obedience, patience, faith and love is very important for them to face the world tomorrow. Teach your children good values. Teach them that having a sound education is vital and precious for the days ahead. A family without God in their lives will have many unsolved problems. The family who does not know God will have weak faith and no hope for the future.

There is no hope for families if they continue with verbal and physical abuse. There is no joy and happiness if physical trauma and emotional abuse persist. A marriage breakdown and divorce can end up with a very unhappy and traumatised family relationship. Having a healthy family is a gift from God which the family must work hard to maintain.

Families are precious gifts given to us by God from birth. Families are priceless. You will make mistakes, but you will need to forgive one another for your own peace of mind. Forgiving one another is very important for the family to move forwards in peace, love and unity. Holding grudges will only hurt you more. As families you need to learn to release any hurt. You need to let go of it and forgive. Let love build your faith and hope for the future for the better. No one in the family should ever accept physical abuse. It could cause emotional and mental trauma.

Conflicts will come but it is how you and your family deal with those conflicts that matter. Despite the unprecedented and uncertain times the world is facing today, there is always hope for families. Love is patient and kind so build your home on true love. Let your marriage be for true love. Parents should continue to teach their children the principles of living a good life. Parents should continue to show love to their children and children should continue to show love to their parents. Parents should be treated with love and be well cared for, as when they are gone, then we will know their full value. We should appreciate their full value when they are alive.

I do not have parents as both of my parents have passed on, so I am experiencing what it is to be without parents. It is like there is always an empty space in a part of my heart. Many of you without parents can testify to this type of feeling.

My siblings and I were blessed to have both parents alive until we all reached adult life. For this, we are very grateful to God. I know of many people whose parents died when they were still in their childhood days.

It is a good thing for parents to teach their children good morals and teach them about love.

When parents are gone, then the love can continue in the home circle, and be circulated in the community. It takes a village to raise a child. If this saying is being practised in many communities, then the world would have many families who are able to survive in the world today. The family can only survive if they put love above everything because God is love. This is why I always believe that, despite money giving us comfort, love will help families stay together in unprecedented times. Even when parents are gone, siblings will be able to continue the running of a good family once the principles of a good family are instilled in their lives. The good teachings of our parents will never leave our hearts and minds. It is also important to have good teachers in school with good morals and good educational values. This will also help children to stay focused on the good teachings of life.

It is vital that we teach our children the dangers of peer pressure as most times children who adhere to peer pressure end up going down the wrong path. Both children and teachers need to look out for the bullies who like to pressure others into doing things they would like to be done. In most cases, these are usually things that would get someone into trouble. Children who adhere to peer pressure usually go against family teachings and this can become a problem in the family circle.

It is vital for parents to have conversations with their children daily to find out how they did at school, how their day was and if there were any issues. Doing this frequently will help your children realise that you care for them, and you are interested in their wellbeing. This will give them the courage to discuss any issues they might be facing at school.

Having family get-togethers is another way of keeping the family together. Giving each other small gifts is another way of showing love in the family. The family getting together for morning devotions is a way of motivating families on the inspirational side. Loving your neighbours as yourself is another way of family survival. Helping one another makes the bond of love stronger. Strong family bonding is a way of helping the family stand strong in the uncertain times ahead of us.

Every family should be like a beacon of light in the community. Families should live a life so the good in that family will reflect on the community. It does not have to be about riches, fancy houses, fancy cars, etc. It can be about your smile or your kindness to others. It can be about the way you greet people in the community. It can be about the way you are always willing to help others. Let people's lives be touched with something good you do. They might not say it, but the good you and I do will go a long way in the lives of many people.

There will always be ups and downs but by trusting God, there will always be hope for today's family. Keep the cord secure in the family. The cord of love will bind your family together.

For family survival, families need to pray and try hard to maintain strong bonds with each other. Family is one of the most precious treasures in our lives that some people take for granted. It is important to cherish and protect it.

Communication is the key to maintaining strong bonds with your family. Take time to talk to your loved ones regularly. Ask them how they are doing. Share your own experiences with them. Be honest and open in your conversations. Don't be afraid to express how you feel.

Secondly, try to spend time together regularly, whether it's by organising family meals or family vacations. Make sure to plan moments where you can all come together and enjoy each other's company. Additionally, be tolerant, be humble, be kind and be respectful towards each other.

We all have our own opinions, but it is important to respect those of other family members. Even if we don't always agree, don't forget to show gratitude towards your family members. Tell them how much you appreciate them and what they mean to you. Small acts of appreciation can make all the difference in maintaining a close and loving relationship with your loved ones.

I pray and hope that all families in the world can adapt to these tips which will be helpful in maintaining strong bonds.

Always remember that family is a source of strength and support, and it is important to cherish and protect our families.

Remember attitudes have the power to make us either happy or make us sad.

Let us be trustworthy, loyal, respectful and kind to our families. Show them love and kindness and care for each other. Don't let negativity creep into the family circle.

Some families don't invite families over because they may find it difficult to find the money. Even some families that may have money do not invite families over. Your get-togethers don't have to be expensive. You can make it simple and cheap, yet enjoyable. A walk in the park. A picnic in the park or the garden. A walk on the beach. Some outdoors games. A day out to the cinema, window shopping, and so much more. These simple things can help to keep the family away from long hours on electronic gadgets.

Some people find it time-consuming to call families but find time to call friends. Most of the time, in difficulties, your family will be there first for you. In some cases, your friends will be there first but most cases your family. Your families are precious gifts given to us by God. Cherish your families. Families are not here forever. Enjoy life with them to the fullest. In good and bad times, let us cherish our families.

It is important for children to treat their parents with love and respect and the same goes for the parents to treat their children with love and respect.

There are benefits of being a teacher in your community. You experience the joy and pride of seeing students learn and grow and celebrating their accomplishments.

Other than parents, teachers have arguably the biggest influence on a child's life. The visible results you'll see from them are guaranteed to send you home with a sense of pride. Teachers have a significant impact on the achievements of many people.

Preparing them to be successful global citizens and ignite in them a desire to excel in school and life is one of the most important responsibilities we have as parents, teachers, caregivers and educators.

We must encourage them to participate in group activities that allow them to interact with others in a positive and supportive way.

Most of all, let God come first in the family life. Love will be the answer to all family situations because God is love. Let love continue to keep your heart happy.

Talk with your children. Having free and uninterrupted communication with your children is of paramount importance. It lays the foundation for a healthy parent–child relationship and enables parents to understand their children's needs, concerns and aspirations. Through open communication, parents can establish trust, foster emotional connections and provide a safe space for their children to express themselves. This helps in building a strong bond based on mutual respect and understanding.

Furthermore, free communication allows parents to guide their children effectively, offering support and guidance when needed, and addressing any issues or challenges that may arise. It also promotes the development of essential life skills such as effective problem-solving, decision-making and conflict resolution. By maintaining open lines of communication, parents can stay attuned to their children's development, ensure their wellbeing, and nurture their emotional and psychological growth.

Interrupted communication can hinder the parent–child relationship and have adverse effects on a child's overall development. When communication is hindered, children may feel unheard, misunderstood or neglected, leading to feelings of isolation or frustration. They may struggle to express their thoughts, emotions or concerns, potentially leading to suppressed feelings or acting out behaviour.

Additionally, interrupted communication can limit the flow of important information, preventing parents from gaining insight into their children's experiences, relationships and challenges. This lack of understanding can strain the parent–child bond and make it difficult for parents to provide the necessary support and guidance their children need. Consequently, it is crucial for parents to prioritise uninterrupted communication, ensuring they are actively present and attentive when engaging with their children, so they can foster a strong and nurturing relationship that promotes their child's overall wellbeing and growth.

Hope for the World

Despite everything going on around the world, there is hope.

Once you and I have true love within our hearts, we will believe that there is hope for the world. To have strong hope in things to come or to have strong hope in whatever you believe in is a good thing. The gift of hope is an amazing and divine gift.

Everyone in the world is praying and hoping for a world where people can live as one and a world where love can triumph.

We are living in a world of constant fear. People's hearts are failing them for fear. Everywhere we go there is always something on the news about the different things that are happening. Many people are hungry. Millions are homeless. Millions are depressed or fighting hard to get out of either depression or some form of addiction. Anxiety and stress are prevalent in today's society. Is there hope? The answer is yes. There is hope for the future. There is hope for the people.

Allow true love to live within your heart and you will be able to increase hope within your heart and mind which is a powerful thing.

Try not to stress too much about the past. Only think more about the good memories of the past. The important thing is to believe there is hope for the future and hope for the world.

Believe in hope. Believe in yourself. Believe in love and believe in God.

Everyone has hope in different things. Some people have hope for a better life. Some people have hope for a better world. Some people have hope in the promises of God. This is called religious hope. Millions of people hope for a better world because they will be able to live more peacefully and lovingly.

We should be happy with what we have. Giving is a wise attribute which will make us happy.

Encouragement to others is like bringing joy to the soul. Challenges in life give us the strength to increase our faith in these unprecedented times. Faith is needed to help get us through the difficult times. When there is nowhere else to turn, we should hang on to faith in God to get us through. Let us remember beyond the midnight comes the morning.

The world needs love to stop the wars and hatred. It is difficult for hate to drive out hate and this is profound. Only love can drive out hatred. Everyone should share more love in the world, then the world would be a better place for us to live in. Greed cannot drive out greed.

A calm sea would never make a good sailor. This is why God sometimes allows difficult times to build our faith to make us stronger.

There are many people suffering in the world today because many people with overflowing cups do not think it wise to share. Many with half cups do the sharing instead. Truthfully, if people spent less money on making themselves look good and spent some money doing good, the world would be a better place. Some people may not agree with this statement, but it is factual.

Our world has a lot of messy churches where some people go to church and haven't heard the sermon. This is either because they were asleep during the sermon, or they were minding someone's else business. Church people should be listening to the sermon, so they can teach others about kindness and help others. Many who go to church today do not practise what they were taught. This chapter of my book may be painful for some church goers, but this is all part of education for hope for the world.

God can use the smallest child to the biggest person to spread love in the world. He can use the poorest person to the richest to spread love in the world.

The same way we weed our garden and clean it up is the same way we need to clean up our lives and try to be a better person each new day. Just as we clean our houses, we should clean up our character and our spiritual lives.

Even the smallest animal can teach us to live in unity and love by the way they do things.

Many of you have so many talented gifts. Use your gifts to make people happy. You have beautiful smiles, use them every day. It would brighten up someone's day and your smiles will help you look younger for a long time. Grumbling often and never being pleased with anything will make your life more unhappy.

It doesn't matter who you are, where you came from, your nationality, or your colour. We can all share love for the world to be a better place.

Let us all work hard and put away the things that are stopping us from entertaining love to the fullest in our hearts and minds. Hatred and grudges are also things that can stop people from sharing love.

Every day we should focus on maintaining a close relationship with God and communicating with him frequently to the significance of staying safe and healthy.

The value of a sound education is incredibly significant to our lives. The importance of road safety must be emphasised, reminding us to be cautious and mindful when using the roadways.

Helping our community to increase the number of activities and learning how to relieve stress is a way of helping many young people reduce mental deterioration. Mental health is especially important today, so looking out for each other's mental health should be increased.

I pray that many people heal from the things they don't speak about.

I saw my sister Doris shared a very motivational and inspiring message on Facebook and I decided to share it with you. This is what she wrote:

> *What consumes your mind controls your life. Focus on God, not the storm that is before us right now. True faith*

is keeping your eyes on God. If the world around you seems to be falling apart, listen to God, not your insecurities. Rely on God, not your own strength. Look the seemingly hopeless circumstances in the face and ask the Lord to anchor us in the truth that he will have the last word.

Rather than giving way to our emotions and fear, watch God send that strong wind from the east and divide that raging Red Sea that is before us and we will walk right through just like the Israelites. They went through on dry ground, with a wall of water on their right and on their left. Oh yes! Jumping for joy, shouting and giving praise to the highest God who promises to never leave nor forsake us. So, today we will stand still and see the salvation of the Lord that he will provide for us today and always.

God is not in a hurry, but we are, and that's why we're sometimes so stressed. We're sometimes anxious, burnt out, restless and frustrated.

You and I need to tone it down, relax and be still in knowing that God's timing is perfect. He is the creator, the Almighty, the earth is his and the fullness thereof. He is in total control, no one else is.

So, there's no need for anyone to run ahead of where he's taking us.

I was truly blessed with that small portion of message by my big sister Doris and thought that I must share it. Indeed, our world needs God to help us. Our world needs love. Our world needs prayer. Prayer is a powerful gift given to us by God to ask for what we need. Prayer keeps us communicating with God. Prayer keeps the kingdom of darkness away from our lives and the lives of our family and friends and others out there. Praying to God protects us. We need lots of prayer for the world we are living in. We need prayer to help take hatred away from our world.

Think on these things.

Light at the End of the Tunnel

The grace and mercies of God are new each morning.

I am a Guyanese. Born and raised in my beautiful land Guyana. Cook-up rice is a delicious dish known to all Guyanese. It is a mixture of rice, peas, vegetables and meat. Guyanese know it is one of the favourite dishes for Old Year's Night (New Year's Eve). Jamaicans, I believe, know it as pellow rice.

Good cook-up rice has so many different ingredients mixed up together in the same pot. This is what makes the food so sweet, especially when we add a bit of coconut milk with garlic and cumin, etc.

Looking at the word of God, this is spiritual food that gives us the emotional faith to deal with the difficult times along the education pathway.

There are people who do not like elevators. Some people are afraid of tunnels. Some people are afraid of being in small places. These types of people have a phobia of being in small places. I am not ashamed to say that I am one of those people. The only thing I am not afraid of is walking the narrow path that leads to life eternal.

Despite the uncertain times, millions are still walking the broad road that leads to destruction. There are many religious wars on planet earth because some religions are fighting for power more than fighting for the truth of God.

The Bible tells us that there is no other name under the heavens whereby we may be saved other than the name of Jesus Christ, our lord and saviour and soon coming king. Jesus is the son of God.

We sometimes walk unseen steps. Sometimes we go through dark valleys, sometimes dark tunnels, and dark pathways on planet earth. Sometimes we are afraid. Sometimes we doubt God. Sometimes we worry as we do not know what the future holds. Sometimes we do not know where our next meal is coming from. Have no fear. God promised to provide our daily bread. There is a light shining at the end of every tunnel.

When the train breaks down in the tunnel, we do not throw our tickets through the train window and jump off the train. No, we sit still and pray. We pray and trust God to fix the problem. Then we trust God to do so and take us through the tunnel safely out into the daylight. It is the same as if we were on a plane. It does not matter what problem the plane may be having. We will not jump through the plane window. We sit still and pray or sometimes we will be afraid and forget to pray.

On my trip to Paris with my daughter during Easter of 2023, we travelled by train. I never knew at that time that the train had to go through a tunnel under the sea for twenty-five minutes before getting to Paris. Fifteen minutes after the train left St Pancras station, my daughter mentioned about the undersea tunnel. Oh my. Was I afraid? Oh, you bet I was afraid. I was like a scaredy cat.

Despite the fact I was so scared on the train to Paris, I had no choice but to pray to and trust God.

We need faith and strength in God that no matter what happens, we know that he is our protector and he promised to be with us everywhere we go.

When we reached France from the tunnel under the sea, I was so happy. Fear of the unknown is a terrible thing. Returning to London was a less fearful experience for me because I knew then what to expect regarding the tunnel.

Many discouraging hours will arise before the rainbow of accomplished goals will appear on the horizon. This is my big sister Doris' favourite quote.

I remembered the story of Moses so many times. Those people were afraid of crossing the Red Sea, but they did not have a choice, so they trusted God through the words of Moses, and the Israelites crossed the Red Sea on dry ground. One of my favourite stories in the Bible.

Just imagine an expanse of water was there seconds before the crossing, yet the God of miracles made those Israelites cross the Red Sea on dry ground. What an amazing God.

Every tunnel has an end. Rain does not fall forever, and storm clouds always pass over. There is a silver lining behind every dark cloud.

Nothing in this world is permanent. There are always changes. Your situation can change. You may be down today and up tomorrow. Stay positive. Keep climbing that ladder of success.

There are so many young people who give up easily without trying. Sometimes they may fail one exam and give up. Giving up should never be an option for any failure.

I was down in the valley before God took me to the mountain top. I used to receive help from people when the mountain top used to seem like a distance far away. I worked extremely hard to get to the top. Looking back now, I can see how far I have come with the help of God and everyone God used to help me up the mountain. There were times I felt like giving up but decided to press on. I could not have done it without God on my side.

I know God was with me all the time. It was the same for every one of you who were in the same situation before you accomplished your dream goals.

Without the knowledge of the word of God, we would not be able to stand the test of time. We are living in uncertain times. Without education, our children will not be able to get good jobs that will help them in these times when prices are rising for everything.

Get your children educated as much as possible. You will not regret it. They will not regret it.

My Reasons for Writing This Book

- It is a joy to share my knowledge with others.
- I write this book because there are many people who sometimes believe that getting to the top is impossible.
- I want to remind everyone that they should stand for what they believe they can achieve.
- I want to let people know they should never doubt their capabilities.
- I want to remind everyone that they have the willpower to make it in life.
- I want to advise everyone that they should never let anyone tell them that they cannot achieve their academic goals.
- I want to encourage people to keep studying and working hard for success.
- The most important thing is that giving up should never be an option where education is concerned.
- I would like for everyone to know that falling does not define them, but it is how they rise to greater heights that defines them.
- My most important reason is to inspire and motivate others to keep studying and climbing the ladder of education success.

- My motto is never stop studying as there is always something new to learn. There is always room for improvement.
- Everyone won't be able to become doctors, lawyers, ministers, presidents, etc., but whatever and whoever you choose to be, do it at your best. Aim for the highest heights in whatever you choose to accomplish.
- We all have our own dreams and aspirations, so aim high and go for it. Give it your best.

Acknowledgements

First, I would like to give thanks to almighty God for giving me the wisdom and knowledge to write this book. I thank God for the vision he has given me to be able to come up with the contents of the chapters of this book.

Thanks to the publishing team for accepting my previous two books for publishing. Thanks for your support and cooperation throughout the publishing process. The entire team has been amazing, and I have no doubt you will be amazing with the publishing process of this book.

Thanks to my daughter Crystal Trudy Johnson who has encouraged and supported me to keep writing as it has become one of my favourite free time activities if I am not working, going to church, choir practice or watching a movie. My daughter is very legal when it comes to writing books. She usually tells me not to write anyone's name in my books without consulting them first etc. Crystal works at a law firm and she is always going by the law book. Serious lawyer she is. So, I must get things right. I am so proud of her and thankful to God for having her in my life.

Thanks to everyone who has supported me with the purchasing of my previous books, and I look forward to your continuing support. Thanks for your amazing book reviews.

Thanks to Amazon and the other online sales stores who are selling my previous books and will be selling this book. I appreciate it.

Special thanks to my sister Doris Anetha Shelto-McLennon who helped me with some of the information to write the first half of my book blurb. She is particularly good at writing. She always writes inspiring articles on Facebook, but she's never actually written a book. I encourage her to do so.

My sister Doris runs a community activities programme and children's education is on the agenda. Every weekend she runs children's classes which are very inspiring and motivating.

Special thanks to Tammy Griffith, who is no longer with us. Tammy passed on a few years ago. She was an amazing singer and she was an amazing writer. Tammy wrote two books. The name of her first book is *Wonderful Words* and her second book is *Think Positive*.

I read Tammy's books and found them amazing and inspiring. Thanks to Tammy's mother Maureen who sold me the books, as Tammy had already passed on when I bought them. Her books have left positive words on the minds of all who have read them, including me.

In my book, I wrote about survival for the family today. Reading Tammy's books helped me with some of the important tips on family survival. I am very grateful to her for leaving such amazing books for the world to be inspired by.

ACKNOWLEDGEMENTS

Thanks to all my family and friends for the encouraging and motivating messages regarding my books. I do appreciate it from the bottom of my heart, and I am very grateful.

Summary

Sometimes being in the valley of life where you can only dream of getting to the top of the academic ladder can be difficult. It can also be a very frustrating thing. I am that person who has been there once in that emotional arena.

I had always dreamt of having a good life where I could support myself and be able to reach that level of success on the pyramid of education.

It took me years of hard work and dedication to achieve my goals. Sometimes some people achieve their goals quickly because they have the money to be able to get higher education whenever they want. For me, I know what it is like to struggle and work extremely hard for my goals.

Despite the years of challenging work and intense struggle, I thank God for allowing me to achieve more than that for which I prayed. I dreamt big but miraculously, my dreams were achieved to a higher level than I could have imagined. My encouragement to every younger person is to dream and aim for the moon. If you fall, you will fall amongst the beautiful stars. Do not think about giving up because it should never be an option if you really need to gain success on the academic ladder.

My motto is never stop studying as there is always something new to learn every day.

I hope you enjoyed reading the contents of my amazing book and I really hope you will be inspired and motivated.

I am looking forward to seeing your reviews after reading my book. Thank you in advance for your support and I wish you all the best in your future endeavours.

www.ingramcontent.com/pod-product-compliance
Lightning Source LLC
Chambersburg PA
CBHW071404080526
44587CB00017B/3177